By The Way...

Collection of Published
Poetry
Fiction
Inspirational Prose
Light Verse and Humor

By Virginia Norris Rhoades
Cover by Chuck Rhoades
Photography by William Rhoades

By The Way...

Virginia Norris Rhoades

Copyright © 2007
All Rights Reserved

Published By:
Brentwood Christian Press
4000 Beallwood Ave.
Columbus, Georgia 31904

Contents

Acknowledgements 5

Foreword 6

Preface 7

I. Poetry 9

II. Fiction 39

III. Inspirational Prose 57

IV. Light Verse and Humor 83

Index 97

Acknowledgements

I gratefully extend appreciation to my graphic artist son Chuck as illustrator and to son William for his photography, and to computer expert Kelsey Kempker for her typing and editing assistance.

Credit is given to the following publishers represented in this collection: *Mature Years*; *Purpose*; *Standard*; *Mature Living*; *St. Joseph's Messenger*; *The Saturday Evening Post*; *Farm and Ranch*; *The Gem*; *Grit*; *The Miraculous Medal; Lifeprints*; *The Improvement Era*; *St. Anthony Messenger*; *Time of Singing*.

FOREWORD

In my own life journey I am indebted to all who have had a positive influence on me. It is my hope that I may effectively evidence the spiritual shaping that I continue to experience.

We know that "Jesus wept" (Luke 19:41; John 11:35). I am confident that he also smiled and laughed, and that he shared the joy of those whose lives he touched with miracles.

In my writing I have shared some of the moments in my own spiritual growth. In this limited collection of selected previously published work I note some of the milestones of experience that have marked my progress as I continue to learn through experiences as deep as sorrow, as bright as the sunlight of happiness, as exciting as discovery, as challenging as the uncertainties of each tomorrow.

I invite you to join me on these pages of my journey.

VNR

PREFACE

Christ tells us, "I am the way, and the truth, and the life. No one comes to the Father except through me…" (John 14:6 NRSV).

We each make our journey of life on our own path, yet there is one divine model for us all to follow. It is *by the way* that Jesus taught and exemplified in all that he represented as the Son of God.

To believe truly is to act upon our belief as Christians sharing our faith from the fullness of our spirit. With this awareness I would offer one prayer to structure our lives as believers praying together:

Our Heavenly Father,
We thank you for the coming of your son Jesus;
Strengthen us in following Christ's teachings and
Help us reflect the
Presence of the Holy Spirit in the
Lives we live.
                        In Christ's name we pray,
                        Amen

Part I

Poetry

New Vision

Through the windows of sight
I focused my trust, believing
All made visible to my receiving
Sufficient to guide my way.

And then a stumbling
Robbed my faith. Dark misery
Closed me in, my soul made mute.
    Long I was lost, until
    I felt there drift like
    Mist upon my spirit, palpably
    A presence, soundless as
    Stroking of fur, healing me
    Of fears, leading me to know
    Unspoken words, power invisibly
    Linked to being, making me whole.

If such is the language of God,
I shall go humbly in all my seeking,
Knowing that in His Keeping
I need no greater faculty.

Not By Bread Alone

I walked upon the mountain,
The world was at my feet,
In a pattern laid by distance,
Remote and fair and neat.

I breathed of rarest freedom
And drank of constant peace;
Upon the tableland of height
Was spread contentment's feast.

Removed from deepest chaos
Where I had walked below,
Sustained by an hour's brief retreat,
A loftier view to know,

Enough to last my journey back,
On familiar ground I found:
I who took the valley up
Could bring the mountain down.

Behold!

Where the rainbow's arc
Touches the ground,
'Tis said a pot of gold
May be found.

I've not seen riches
In coins of gold
Gleaned from the myth
Repeated of old.

But I've seen in the rain
Sun's rays filtering through,
With layers of colors
Curving to view.

Could there be greater
Treasure, rare to the eye,
Than such lavish beauty,
God's covenant in the sky?

To God

Upon the fertile field I look
And sense that You are there;
Within the rippling of a brook
I feel that You are there.

When I witness flood and quake
With fixed and hollow stare,
God, strengthen my heart in horror's wake
To trust Your presence everywhere.

MARY

God's great mystery:
    Angel Gabriel, his messenger,
    sent to me, a virgin,
    saying I should become
    mother of Christ, the Messiah.

Yet I could not foresee
    his agony at Gethsemane,
    the fatal march to Calvary,
    his death at thirty-three.

My tears, my prayers…
    my eyes opened to
    God's victory…
    Christ's resurrection:

The promise of life
    eternal for all
      believers…
I rejoice in the
    Father's blessing.

GLIMPSES OF GOD

Longing to see the
    face of God
I looked in vain,
Needing some beacon of light,
Some sign a sure
Witness to his presence.

I watched a night
    nurse easing a patient's pain,
Saw a day school
    toddler sharing his pushcart,
A wheelchair-bound man reach
    out to break a friend's fall.

Christ's words came alive…
    "Love one another"
And I recognized
God's image,
Brightly shining.

God in Christ

Forgiving God,
Sending His Son at last,
Supreme love, hope

Need we wonder, Christ
Speaking for children…
Having lived Jesus, the child?

God's Son armored with
Honor, frustrating enemy,
Buffeting evil

Christ's promise, life
Eternal, through belief…
By God's grace

Thirty-three years,
Christmas to Easter…Christ's
Life, mission fulfilled

DESTINED TO GOD'S PURPOSE

"Slow of speech," no excuse
For Moses…projected
By God to lead

Ignoring God's call…
In the great fish belly
Jonah learned to obey

Job, tormented in
Loss…humbled to God's will,
His soul restored to hope

Sold into slavery,
Redeemed to God's service
…Joseph in Egypt

Haunted by his sins,
David in repentance
Gaining God's mercy

Wracked with guilt,
His denial of Jesus…
Peter to become Christ's rock

Saul the persecutor,
Blinded…transformed by
The Lord to apostle Paul

Holy Week Haiku

Palms waving, children's
Hosannas…praising Jesus…
In love's innocence

How blessed are we…heirs…
First sacred Communion…bread…
Wine…Christ's Last Supper

Peter's denial
Of Christ…his shame we share…when
We falter in faith

Glare of cross…darkness
Of tomb…come forth, our hope…lead
Us to light…life…love

Savior's death…passage…
Resurrection…triumph…Christ's
Truth…eternal life

Haiku…In Spirit

One mustard seed of
Faith burgeoning to flower…
Nurtured by belief

    Opening lilies
    Greeting Easter…white trumpets
    In silent worship

No coins of gold, earth
End of rainbow…treasure, God's
Covenant in sky

    Ant busy gleaning:
    Evidence…now is the
    Only time we have

REFLECTIONS

only after I
        fell…your pain
                became real to me

a closed heart
        makes aliens
                of us all

nest building thrush
        straw upon straw
                ritual of trust

last fruit on
        shaken tree…
                clinging hope

Church carillon
        tangled traffic
                silent oak

shriek of siren
        blocks away…helpless
                to help, I pray

more agonizing
        than pain, awaiting joy—
                unsure of its name

THE FENCE IS BROKEN

The fence is broken,
The lamb is out…
      The wolf waits…
Too late for mending.

PATH OF CONTRITION

Esau's birthright sold...
    yearning for love, he pleads
        "bless me...also, father!"
(Genesis 27:38)

David confessing
    treachery, begs God:
        "blot out my transgressions."
(Psalm 51:1)

Prodigal's anguished
    cry "I have sinned...."
        Finds father forgiving.
(Luke 15.21)

Thief on the cross, his
    spirit opened to Christ,
        "Jesus, remember me...."
(Luke 23:42)

The good of guilt?
    repentance...forgiveness
        soul's peace.

TRANSFORMATION

As a seed encased in
> its hard shell lies
> barren until planted
> in fertile soil,

So the lost soul
> remains lifeless, until
> filled with the saving
> grace of the Holy Spirit.

REGENERATION

Prayer of the contrite heart:
Take this broken vessel, Lord,
And mend it for your use;
Gather its fragments and seal
Its fractured seams until, made
Pure and refined as by your first
Creation, it stands prepared
To pour forth the saving balm
Of your love, made perfect
In Christ.

SEARCHING

I felt an invitation
When I heard a Church bell ring,
And longed to hear God's voice
As I listened to choirs sing;

I walked a lonely garden,
Sensed Christ's presence there,
And found divine communion
In the silent comfort of prayer.

FAITH'S WITNESS

You walked there in the teeming city,
Erect, sure, with measured tread,
Chin up and facing straight ahead;
You halted, awaited the gentle tug
Beside you, nor did the smug,
The tired, the seeking faces,
The many steps to many places
Distract you from attentive waiting;
And then your signal, with noise abating,
You followed with unfaltering feet
Your leashed companion across the street;
Deep in your world devoid of sight
Lives a faith that conquers night.

"...for the one who believes"

As the vessels of oil were
    miraculously replenished
    over and over for the
    impoverished widow
    seeking help from
    the prophet Elisha,
So faith nourishes the
    soul of the seeker who
    hearkens to the words
    of Christ: "All things
    can be done for the one
    who believes."

                    (Mark 9:23)

LIVING & BELIEVING

People who say life is *too* short to:
…hold grudges…seek revenge…worry
about bad decisions…fret over
small things…feel guilty for past mistakes,
Though sounding rather high-minded,
seem to harbor a certain
doubtful outlook beneath their
bold, assertive words.

Life is *too* long, I'd say, not to:
…practice faith…be forgiving…
forget much…remember the best…
…grant patience its due…
give more credence to good
than bad…and, with God's blessing,
be able to age without
becoming low-spirited.

Proximity

How easy it seems to speak knowingly,
A worthy solution to find,
When the problem is hypothetical,
And can be firmly resolved in the mind;

But strong are conflicting emotions
That can challenge the heart and soul,
When the place is here, the time now,
To be fair and wise and bold.

Heart's Reach Unlimited

Who can say love
    favors only the young?
Late love can dawn
    fresh as a new morning,
Strong as the bonds
    of ancient myth;
Heart's reach is
A touch, a smile, across
    the breach of time;
Time never shared before
Together;
Time sharpened to the
    sting of new tears
And laughter rippling
    across years
Never known together –
        Until now.

Stepmother to Small Daughters

Into their loss she came meeting their need

With words of warmth and hands of love to feed

The bread of hope; into silken halos she brushed their hair

And fashioned dresses for them to wear;

She's woven with her faith the lost pattern of their

Believing, strong and secure—together grown

In love, these not her flesh, now born her own.

AUTUMN TO REMEMBER

Ecclesiastes 3:1a; 3:11a, KJV

"To everything there is a season..."
"He hath made every thing beautiful in his time..."

A train whistle, like a
Mourning dove's call, reaching
Far across country afternoon
Stillness; a mountain
Ablaze with the
Fire of fall foliage;
Harvest time and syrup mills,
Dray horse treading the circles
Of the cane crushers, squeezing
Juice for the cauldrons, molasses
Boiling in the making;
Apples rendering their
Ripeness to nectar
And sauce and apple butter
To stock the winter pantry.

Church Attendance

What?...a lively rabbit
      far from field and native habit
      where cottontails hop at dawn,
      poised on the clipped church lawn.

Surely he knows he can be seen,
      brown tones upon a canvas of green;
      his security's need
      depends on camouflage and speed.

Yet in the midst of urban sound,
      as if knowing hallowed ground,
      he observes me with innocent eye,
      belonging here as much as I.

LOOK UP

Behold a sky of stars,
Perfect performers in night
Concert conducted by moon-
light,
Playing *soundless bars
Of symphony* across Light-
Years as near as sight.

LOVE, UNITY, AND PEACE…
a strong trio of words
weakened only when
overused but under-practiced.

JUST AS SAWDUST

Just as sawdust
reveals the soft
side of hardwood,
So forgiveness can
make gentle the
hardest heart.

LEGEND

From tongue to tongue the echo
Almost lost but ever heard anew: Know
This—past all glib persuasion,
Beyond the doubter's sharp denial—
There is no virtue without temptation,
No honor without trial.

Part II

Fiction

The Lemon Yellow Dress

The car door closes with a sharp, heavy click and eleven-year old Penny watches her father and Gwen walk up the rock path leading to the terrace.

"Coming Penny?" her dad asks over his shoulder. Gwen calls back, "We'll get the camera."

Penny, her small round face clouded in a frown that shadows her delicate features and clear blue eyes, stands absently fingering her velvet belt, waiting for the two of them to go into the house. Turning, she walks rapidly beyond the summerhouse and darts behind a hedge, her long brown hair bobbing on her shoulders. With heart pounding as it did when she was sitting at the piano on stage in the high school auditorium only an hour ago, she hurries along the path. Vines are becoming thickly entangled, brushing against her. She looks down at the dress she is wearing, hating it, the dress Gwen selected. It binds her body like a rope. The past months since her father married Gwen seem forever.

Thoughts pepper her steps as she remembers past long walks in the sundappled mornings, trail rides on weekends. Her dad never seems to have time for these things any more. When she reminds him, he catches his breath as if he just thought of something unexpected. "Sure, Penny, we must go riding again soon. Maybe Gwen can join us."

She pushes forward recklessly, muttering to herself. "I guess Gwen doesn't like horses."

Briars growing in ragged clumps snatch at her like claws across the bulky skirt; she feels wicked pleasure knowing Gwen picked out the monstrous thing for the recital. It was hanging in her room when she came home from school today. Just like that. Nothing like the way her mother had prepared, letting her choose the material, the pattern and everything. What dreamy dresses her mother could make, the waist fitting so snugly, the colors so bright and happy.

Tears are springing suddenly, swimming across her vision. Heedlessly she plunges through the underbrush. All at once she is in a slight clearing and before her are yellow heads of dandelions bobbing like cheerful dancers in a gentle breeze. She stoops to gather some.

Inside the cemetery she walks slowly past weathered markers dating their family history back for generations until she stands beside the newest one. Only the date carved into the headstone reveals the passage of three years. Carefully she places her wildflowers. For a long time she stands, with nothing but the wind seeming alive around her. The little clump of dandelions begins to wilt in the warm, late afternoon sunlight. A sudden puff of spirited air whips at her dress, swirling it out in flag-like folds, but it becomes blurred as she blinks away the stern finality of the letters on the headstone.

She is remembering the events of another recital day and how different that afternoon was. Her mother, proud and radiant, was hugging her neck and whispering playfully, "Don't tell anyone, but I think you are the star performer." She felt herself glowing in a sky-blue dress that plunged delightfully to the floor, with yards of ruffles and a gardenia corsage.

Suddenly she blurts aloud, "Why did you die and leave me?"

With abrupt, swift insistence the breeze flares out her dress, inviting Penny to reconsider it. She watches as sunlight dances over the tiny pearl buttons on the lemon-yellow bodice, drawing her attention upward. A black butterfly, in startling contrast, silky brilliant, lights upon a button. Holding her breath, she reaches up to close her hands over it.

At that moment a voice sounds in the distance. Her dad is calling her. Turning, she runs from the cemetery, back up the path, ignoring the jagged masses now that tear across her skin and her clothes.

At last, flushed and out of breath, she stands before him. "Where have you been, Penny?" he is asking. "We wanted to get some snapshots before the sun sets."

"Looks as if she's been out for a walk," Gwen speaks quietly, seeing her discomfort, "Here, I brought a brush. Thought you might want to touch up your hair...the wind is playful today." Tall and graceful, with sandy, short hair and deep gray eyes, Gwen approaches. "My goodness, you've scratched your arms and legs!"

"Oh, they don't hurt." Penny rubs her arms, denying the painful stinging.

Gwen's eyes sweep over her, noticing the ugly tear in her skirt.

Penny gasps as she spies it, too.

Leaning over, Gwen examines the fabric. "I doubt it will show in the picture. When we go inside I'll mend it."

"Mend it?" blurts Penny.

"Yes," Gwen is explaining. "I made it. I should be able to mend it, shouldn't I? And she smiles as she watches closely the astonished face before her.

"You? You mean——you can sew? You made this dress?" Penny stammers, dropping her eyes in confusion.

"Yes, I enjoy sewing, but I didn't want to let you know I made your dress. I was afraid you might not like it.

I thought the yellow would be pretty with your dark hair."

"How did you know my size?" Penny questions, noticing for the first time how smoothly the velvet belt circles her slender waist.

"Oh, that was easy. I fitted it by your other dresses."

"But my mother always made my dresses. I thought…"

Gwen's hand is on her arm. "You miss your mother terribly, don't you, Penny?"

She can do no more than nod, tears choking her voice.

"My mother died when I was seven. I know how lost and lonely you can feel."

Swallowing hard, Penny stares at the ground.

"I knew you were closing me away. I hoped the dress would make a difference…if you liked it, it could bring us closer together." Her voice is little more than a whisper. Looking up, Penny is surprised to see tears in her eyes, too.

And then she feels her dad's arms around her. Reaching out, he draws Gwen into their circle. Passing her hand lightly over her eyes, Gwen straightens, looking into her husband's face. Turning, she is saying to Penny, "I enjoyed your piano solo. I bet your dad agrees with me that you were the prettiest girl there. We're both proud of you." She pauses, adding, almost shyly, "We love you very much."

Penny's heart is racing. "I'm sorry I ran away." Her thoughts fly to the wilted flowers in the cemetery. She knows tomorrow she will carry fresh flowers, but she won't go alone. As if her mother is speaking to her, she realizes that love doesn't die in death. It lives in everything that brings joy. In sharing love, it lives for always.

She looks at Gwen. "I'm glad you made the dress for me."

"Say, who's ready for a picture?" Her dad is focusing the camera.

Slowly she runs her fingers over the torn skirt, desperately wanting it whole again. She catches her breath as a gust of wind swirls under the fluffy folds of bright yellow organdy. And suddenly—the ugly, briar torn dress is beautiful.

A Light in the Night

Flushed with the successful closing of my first real estate transaction as a new broker, I felt exhilarated but exhausted. All I could think of was pushing back from my desk, hopping in my car, and heading for the mountains to the little retreat cabin my husband and I had bought the previous year, celebrating *his* first bonus.

No need to tell anyone I was going. My husband was out of town and the anticipation of breezing up the interstate, getting farther and farther from the city traffic, crowded all other thoughts from my mind.

Turning off onto a two-lane state road, I felt the speed demon urge of the open highway fade, and I relaxed enough to enjoy the scenery. The mountains always inspired me, with every changing season bringing a new vista of beauty—winter snowfall, autumn leaf splendor, summer lush greens, spring blossoms—dotting the heights in cascades of color.

Memories floated back as I turned onto the narrow gravel road leading upward, until I began to sense fresh mountain air ridding me of all I was fleeing from—urban heat, traffic noise, telephones ringing. I opened my window, turned off the air-conditioner, and clicked off the CD.

As I pulled into the little cleared area by the cabin, my eyes searched upward to the heights that seemed like encircling arms of giants cradling this spot hidden from the access road. In the afternoon hush, I thought of my father and how we had trekked up to the pinnacle of the mountain near our home when I was a child. It became a cherished ritual on weekends. When we reached the top, breathless but triumphant, Dad would stand solemnly surveying the valley below us and say, "Being here always makes me feel nearer to the Lord. As one little speck in His universe, I am in awe of His dominion over all things. I'm reminded of Psalm 46:10, 'Be still, and know that I am God! I am exalted among the nations, I am exalted in the earth'."

I loved climbing the mountain, but I could never think of myself as a speck in the universe. I didn't rebel openly against my father and his firm faith, reading the Bible, going to church, praying. Yet by the time I finished college, I was convinced my mother's advice was right—to follow my ambition and be glad that, as a woman, I had opportunities far greater than her generation ever had. The spirit of gaining success in a competitive world became top priority.

A sudden clap of thunder broke my reverie of times past. In moments I was caught in the full force of a mountain storm, the kind that can drown a summer day in a drenching rainfall. The sky darkened and an ominous darkness eclipsed the sun behind the towering peaks. The storm did not hit and run, chasing out pockets of heat and blowing away quickly to refresh out valleys. It raged with unrelenting fury. I sat hoping for a chance to get out of the car.

Lightning slashed across the face of the nearest ridge. Galvanized in fear, I knew it was no time to try to walk to the door of the cabin. Finally, I realized, as an eerie darkness settled over the valley below, that I'd better head back to the city. I started down the long drive, remembering as I did that there was a small stream I had to cross.

My headlights picked up the sight of rushing water. No need to worry though; the stream was shallow. I drove slowly but steadily into the whirl of water. Without warning, a sudden gush of fresh downpour rushed under the car, throwing it out of control and slamming me forward. My head hit the steering wheel.

When I regained consciousness, I noticed that everything was quiet except for the active gurgle of the still-swollen stream. What time could it be? In the dark, I couldn't see my watch. Maybe I should call my husband. I reached for my cell phone. To my horror, I couldn't find it. *Must have left it at the office in my hurry to leave. I'll get out and try to walk down the road where I can use the nearest neighbor's phone.*

When I tried to open my door, the car teetered unsteadily. I reached to turn on the ignition so the headlights could show me where I was. No luck. I was stranded in a stalled-out car, with no way to call anyone. When I tried to shift positions, the car seemed to shift too. What was causing this?

Panic pinched me motionless, afraid to move. How long I sat there I don't know. All I could do was keep telling myself, "Sit still, sit still." Then, I recalled Dad's favorite verse from years gone by. "Be still, and know that I am God."

How could God not know that I was here? I needed help. I couldn't call on a God I had almost forgotten, a Sunday God for people at church time. Childhood bedtime prayers didn't seem to fit my desperate situation right now.

What was that? A crackling of underbrush nearby set my heart pounding. *A bear?* The area was home to much wildlife. Bears roamed freely. Then, as swiftly as it had come, it stopped, leaving empty silence again, except for the now subdued murmur of flowing water.

So dark, the deep dark of mountain night with no stars shining. I breathed in shallow expectancy, fear giving rise to despair. My head was throbbing.

There! Something was flashing! A bobbing light approached, and a dog's boisterous barking grew closer, louder. Suddenly, the sound of a man's voice startled me. I jerked my head around and heard,

"Whoa! Don't move, young lady!"

He was near enough now to me to lift the lantern he carried and get a good look at my car. "You stay put. Your front wheels are hanging over a deep ditch. Another foot and you'd have gone over. I'll go for my truck and pull you back onto the roadway. Can you hold on a little longer?"

I closed my eyes and nodded, afraid even to breathe deeply.

When he returned, his dog bounded out of the cab with him, his tail wagging vigorously. His bark sounded like a celebration all the time my car was being pulled back to safety.

Able at last to open my door, I tried to thank the grizzled stranger who had seemed to appear out of nowhere. "What do I owe you for rescuing me?"

Ignoring the question, he said, "Crank it up. Let's be sure you're ready to go."

Eager now to get back home, I listened intently as I turned the ignition key. A cough, a sputter, and then, like a swimmer shaking off a splash of water, the motor caught and began to hum. Relieved, I exclaimed, "I do thank you." Reaching for my handbag, I searched for my billfold.

"Don't thank me. You owe me nothing. I'm glad we found you. I would never have known you were here without Rascal. We went out after the storm to check the pasture fences. He disappeared and then all of a sudden he was back, raising such a ruckus I had to pay attention to him."

The huge, mixed-breed dog stood quietly, wagging his shaggy tail. "You can thank Rascal. His barking led me here." He leaned over, patting the dog's head.

"They're called 'dumb animals'. You couldn't prove that by me. I've seen far too much not to believe in a greater power that nobody can see but never fails to see us and send messengers where they're needed." He paused, stood up straight, his serious face wrinkling into a suggestion of a smile. In the dim light, I imagined his eyes twinkling. "Who's to say the Almighty doesn't send a four-footed angel sometimes?"

Turning, he walked back to his truck, letting Rascal hop in first. "We'll follow you down to the highway, just to be sure you're on your way OK."

As I drove down the drive in the still night that had settled into the coolness of after-storm quiet with only the headlights beaming the way, I felt a strange wonder at this rugged mountaineer. And for the first time in my life, I understood what my father had felt each time we reached the top of the mountain so long ago.

A Good Samaritan

For one flashing moment in fading daylight he saw the truck crest the hill, bearing down on him over the center line. Before his foot could touch the brake or he could turn the steering wheel the crash____

Billy Mc Williams, driving home with his eight year old son Mack, entered a space of nothingness, a space suddenly filled with all the images that he had driven into the recesses of his mind since childhood.

Like a parade of ghosts they moved before him. His father, William Hunter Mc Williams, who gained prominence as the leading trial lawyer in small town Shepherdsville, who dissolved his code of ethics in alcohol and was finally disbarred, becoming known instead as the town drunk. His mother, ever uncritical and patient, who gave up her battle against cancer and died before she ever saw her grandson.

Hating being known as Hunter Mc Williams' son, he became Billy. With single-minded certainty he worked his way through college, graduated with honors, passed his bar exam, and was invited to join a growing firm in the state capital. There he met and married a senator's daughter. They moved to the suburbs, joined a small Church in the community, and started a family.

Billy became an ardent and well-known contributor to many causes, charities, and projects. Heading the building committee at his Church he proudly saw the name Mc Williams placed on the plaque of the stained glass window framing the baptismal font.

Having his name Billy Mc Williams recognized for his contributions and support was a point of high pride for him. Billy became the man to know to endorse any pet project of Church, school, or community. As long as he received credit he met new goals.

It was only after his son started to school and brought home a new set of challenges for promoting his reputation as a man never to be mistaken for the man he remembered his father to be that he felt the burden of his childhood eased from his shoulders.

His wife Carolyn encouraged his many interests and pursued her own as their son reached school age. Support for historical restorations and local theater consumed much of her time. And when Billy began to gain public recognition for his pro bono legal work in behalf of neglected and abused children, she occasionally teased him for needing to be in the limelight all the time making sure his name was always identified with the good things he did.

"Never stop doing helpful things for other people, Honey." She smiled. "I think everyone knows your name by now. Billy Mc Williams is a household word around here."

"Flattery is not needed, Beautiful. Or is it veiled sarcasm?"

"Neither. I just thought..."

"You're trying to tell me something, aren't you? I work too hard to escape the Hunter Mc Williams image. Right?"

"Well-I-I..."

"I don't want our son to repeat his grandfather's mistakes."

"Is that why you wanted to call him Mack and not William Hunter Mc Williams the third?"

"I wanted to keep the family name but I must admit I wanted our son to be his own individual self."

An eerie silence of suspended time fell over the crash scene like the aftermath of thunder.

And then the presence of sirens, police cars, and a gathering of onlookers made the sight a macabre converging of lights in the deepening twilight. Voices, questions punctured the air.

"I saw a man jump out of his car right behind the one that got hit. He ran down into the woods by the road," one driver said, pointing to the spot where the man disappeared.

The driver of the truck was on his feet and walking. Billy was being removed from the driver's side of his car. Two medics hurried in the direction pointed out and heard, "Here, over here." Low-hanging evergreen branches shrouded their view from the road. Following the sound of his voice they found crouched by Mack's side a burly, dark-haired fellow applying pressure to the youngster's hemorrhaging leg.

"Am I glad you guys have come. I couldn't leave him once I found him down here. Good thing I saw it happen. Otherwise, by the time anyone found him here it would have been too late. He was unconscious when I reached him, bleeding like crazy."

When they brought Mack to the ambulance and looked around, the man was nowhere to be seen.

At the hospital Billy regained consciousness to see his wife beside his bed. "Where's Mack?" he whispered hoarsely.

"Down the hall."

"Is he...is he OK?"

Her face drawn, her expression inscrutable, Carolyn replied, "Thank God for the person who found him and stopped the bleeding. That's what saved his life, the doctors said."

"Who was it?" Billy struggled to speak. Taking his hand, his wife squeezed it gently. "That's just it, Billy. No one knows. As soon as the medics arrived and reached Mack, he disappeared."

"We must find out his name."

"I asked the police but they said in the failing light nobody got his license number. He was gone when the emergency crew got Mack to the ambulance."

When Billy was able to walk to his son's room, Mack was asleep. To his father he appeared as defenseless as the squirming infant he had held in his arms the day he was born. He had to touch him. With a rush of relief he felt the pulsing beat of his heart and watched his rhythmic breathing.

A haunting question filled his own chest with a hollow emptiness that demanded an answer. The anonymous person who had saved his son's life. Who was he?

Mack opened his eyes. seeing his father beside him he smiled. "Hi, Dad. Are you OK?"

"Sure. A bad bump on the head. But I'll be all right."

Billy sat down, not wanting to admit the room was beginning to spin. "You know someone found you after the wreck. You remember that?"

"When we got hit, my door flew open. I got out of my car seat and tried to run. I was so scared. And then I saw the blood on my arms and legs and I fell. That's all I remember."

At that moment Carolyn walked in and saw how flushed Billy's face was. She urged him. to go back to his room. "There are more tests to be run tomorrow, Billy. Let's go back so you can lie down. You need to rest."

Billy resisted her suggestion. "Mack can't remember the person who reached him after the crash."

Holding his arm Carolyn said softly, "I'm just glad he found Mack when he did."

"He should be recognized as the hero he is," Billy said, almost in protest. "He saved our son's life, Carolyn."

"Yes, I know. The medics said Mack would have bled to death if no one had found him."

His voice urgent, Billy insisted, "We must thank this man. If we could only know who he is…"

Mack, seeing his father's agitation, grew restless. "Don't worry, Dad. We don't know his name." He paused, his face deeply serious, "But we do know he was a good man."

A good man. Anonymous mercy. Maybe that's really what mattered. Billy McWilliams was a man who found that hard to accept. He believed in giving credit where credit was due and in his surge to success in his life he equally believed in receiving credit for what he did.

He looked at his young son who had so calmly stated what he thought was important. Could he be right? One person acting with no goal of reward, doing an act of bravery, not identifying himself, showing selfless courage when only minutes separated life and death. What was more giving than that?

Recovering in the weeks that followed, seeing his son's vigorous return to play on his Little League team, Billy went through each day with one unanswered question skirting the edge of his mind. Carolyn had written a letter of appreciation that appeared is the local paper. Perhaps the unknown person to whom they felt indebted would identify himself.

No one contacted them. The mystery became an ever-present halo of hope for Billy that he could in some way acknowledge his gratitude.

The week that Mack's Sunday School class read the Bible story of the good Samaritan, he surprised his father with the question, "What was the good Samaritan's name, Dad?"

"Well," Billy hesitated, "I'm not sure."

"Our teacher said no one knows his name. He's just called the good Samaritan because he stopped and saved an injured man beside the road." Suddenly his voice rose as if in discovery, "Maybe that's like the man who saved my life."

Carolyn, listening to them, chuckled, "I think he's right, Billy. His own Good Samaritan. Mack can always remember that name."

When the new season started, Mack's team needed new uniforms. Billy organized the funding project and secured sponsorship from a community hardware store. New equipment he supplied himself, but the record revealed only an Anonymous Donor, with a request that credit go to all the generous volunteers who had helped.

Part III

Inspirational Prose

Out of the Ordinary

Are you ordinary? The word ordinary can describe a person, an occurrence, a situation—anything that the dictionary defines as average, usual, commonplace. This description does not suggest something to be admired, aspired to, experienced with joy and pride.

How often we hear that God chose "ordinary" people to declare his word. Can this be true? Surely no person is ordinary who is called into God's service. And is not every believer called to serve the Lord?

Let us consider what is *not* ordinary:

- No Christian is ordinary, having declared belief in Jesus the Messiah, Son of God. "The one who believes and is baptized will be saved..." (Mark 16:16 a); that person is a believer who strives to live the message of Christ to his disciples, "...make disciples of all nations...teaching them to obey everything that I have commanded you..." (Matthew 28:19-20).
- No work is ordinary that contributes to making the world a better place to inhabit. Remember Christ's words, "...let your light shine...so that (others) may see your good works and give glory to your Father in heaven" (Matthew 5:16).
- No person is ordinary who helps his neighbor in need. Jesus firmly places the commandment before the lawyer who is questioning him, "...you shall love your neighbor as yourself" (Matthew 22:39).
- No day is ordinary that holds one glint of sunlight, one moment of gladness, one strain of music. "This is the day that the Lord has made; let us rejoice and be glad in it" (Psalm 118:24).

- No place is ordinary that holds a spirit of worship. Jesus instructs his disciples, "For where two or three are gathered in my name, I am there among them." (Matthew 18:20).
- No scene is ordinary that inspires reflection. "Let the little children come to me…it is to such as these that the kingdom of God belongs" (Mark 10:14). Jesus admonishes his disciples,"…whoever does not receive the kingdom of God as a little child will never enter it" (Mark 10:15).
- No time is ordinary that challenges us, day by day, to be living proof of the values in which we believe. The risen Christ directs his disciples, "Go into all the world and proclaim the good news to the whole creation" (Mark 16:15).

As Christians we inherit that call to live our beliefs. Yet how often we falter and fail. We even seek the haven of being ordinary. Faced with a tough decision or an intimidating challenge, we waver and yield to external forces that influence what we do.

How easy to say, "I had no choice," in explaining some action taken. We even assume the position of the victim, extend blame to circumstances beyond our control and say we behaved as an ordinary person would be expected to do. We avoid the fact that we always have a choice.

As psychiatrist Viktor E. Frankl, Nazi concentration camp survivor and author of the theory of logotherapy, declares, "…everything can be taken from a man but one thing: the last of the human freedoms—to choose one's attitude in any given set of circumstances, to chose one's own way" (*Man's Search for Meaning*, Touchstone Books, 1984).

It is up to each of us as a believer to grasp the promise of that one freedom that cannot be taken from us:

making our own choices. Only in stepping out of the role of assuming the ordinary do we choose the path of our greatest calling—recognizing and honoring the spirit of God in all of life.

Hidden Handicaps

What growing-up youngster doesn't long for a pony, a real live saddle-up-and-ride pony? With country acres of meadow for grazing, a fresh stream for water, a cozy barn to settle into for evening feeding, my imaginary pony already had everything needed.

All I needed was the pony. With a domestic menagerie of pets to care for already, however, I couldn't convince my parents that I really needed the responsibility of a pony.

Then the unexpected happened. One of my city friends won a Shetland pony in a contest. With no space to keep the prize, the family decided the pony needed a country home.

How could my family refuse a pony that really needed us? That's how Patsy joined us—brown and white and beautiful. In a short time I learned the skill of saddling up, using a currycomb, brushing, and feeding an animal considerably larger than a puppy or a calf.

It was the beginning of a new experience that made summer more fun than ever. I trimmed her long thick mane to keep her cool. I brushed her, cleaned her hooves, and—best of all—we became riding buddies.

I learned how to tighten the cinch enough to keep the saddle secure. This was not her favorite activity, having the saddle girth fastened around her middle. Yet, for racing down the long driveway to the mailbox and for make-believe pony shows the full saddle treatment was necessary. I wore sandals that fit into the stirrups. Summer in Georgia was far too hot for riding boots.

Often we rode without a saddle. Riding bareback, pretending to hunt buffalo, I would hold her mane, hook my legs tightly, and lean far over her side. The purpose was not to be seen as the "hunter" approached the "herd."

Patsy loved that game. She didn't have to wear a saddle with the tight strap binding her. I loved it, too. Going barefoot gave me more control in keeping my balance.

She became so dear to us we let her walk up the steps to the back porch for a tasty treat, an apple or a bit of sugar. We photographed her doing this, a privilege that marked her as special.

There were sour moments, though. Sometimes, for no apparent reason, she'd buck when wearing her saddle. Examination showed nothing wrong with the way it was fitting. One day as we galloped down the drive, she suddenly bucked, flinging me off. Shaken and angered, I whacked her with the reins.

After that, I began riding bareback more. Toward the end of summer she suddenly died. The veterinarian said she had suffered acute indigestion.

I grieved for the loss of Patsy. Learning the cause of her death, I felt guilt and regret. Guilt at having struck her for throwing me when the tight binding of the saddle girth must have been causing her pain. Regret that I had not noticed any problem.

In the years since that childhood experience, I have grown in awareness that everyone is vulnerable, weak, disabled, afflicted, or susceptible in some way. Some handicaps are visible, openly evident; many are not. When I encounter an ugly-acting individual—a rude, surly, disgruntled person—I have to consider that there must be a reason for such an attitude. How do I react to it?

It's not easy to combat bad with good. It's almost a reflex emotion to give tit for tat when we are hurt, insulted, or abused. Or, perhaps worse, we pass along our own pain and frustration to someone else. Remembering my angry response toward my pony when she threw me, unaware of her problem, I try to temper my responses to others.

I think of Christ's words, "In everything, do to others what you would have them do to you" (Matthew 7:12). That's a lot to live by, but simply trying makes many hard circumstances easier to handle.

A Lesson Long Remembered

"Judge not, that ye be not judged. For with what judgment ye judge, ye shall be judged: and with what measure ye mete, it shall be measured to you again."
Matthew 7:1-2 (KJV)

We were playmates, companions in the unspoken balance of equality that children can practice without constraint in a society often dominated by restrictive custom, social pressures, and lopsided unwritten laws.

We were oddly matched. She, at nine, was the youngest member of a large family headed by a strong-willed black mother who occupied a tenant house on a country property owned by my family. I, an only child, was a ten-year old favored with a domestic menagerie of pets and farm animals from which I was gaining a progressive education in the laws of nature.

A school club project in which I raised baby chicks and entered select hen eggs in the county fair gave me good practice in some of the disciplines of responsibility. Part of the cost for winning blue ribbons was the task of keeping the henhouse clean and the nests well settled in fresh pine straw. "Little Dottie" proved a willing helper. We made it fun working together.

When my father and I planned to dam a sturdy little stream into a pond just the size to hold a small home-designed boat, he let me help enough to be able to brag to my mother that "Dad and I are building a dam so we can have a pond for the boat we are making."

It followed easily that when I discovered a saucer-sized mussel in the shallow water of our new pond I could hardly wait to show it to "Little Dottie." It looked like a huge oyster and its dull-toned shell was edged in scallop arcs. If you wanted to see its real beauty, though, you had to approach very quietly and lean over slowly, carefully to observe the gleaming mother-of-pearl interior of its shell as it lay submerged and partially open in the clear water. The slightest sound or stirring of the water and snap! the edges sealed away its pristine secret.

Only Dad and Dottie and I knew of it. The mystery of its appearance had added to its fascination for us. Just so did its disappearance jolt me to a sudden reaction. I blurted to my father when we could not find it one day in its familiar spot, "She took it. Dottie took it. Nobody else knew about it but us."

"Now don't jump to conclusions," he cautioned.

I stayed away from the pond several weeks, trying not to say anything to Dottie about the missing mussel. The day I finally went back, silent, searching, hoping for the mussel's return, I stared into the shallow water to see only two separated shell halves. My mussel had died.

I heard my father gently asking me, "Aren't you glad you didn't accuse your friend wrongly?" When he said that, I felt chastened by his words.

It wasn't until I was much older and had witnessed the virulent power of divisive inherited racial prejudices that I realized how fortunate I was that my wise father had referred to "Little Dottie" uncompromisingly as my friend.

Deadly Fire

As a grade-schooler I stood by the country roadside near my home and watched a woods fire fanned by the winds of March blaze across a neighbor's acreage.

Just home from school I had heard my mother answer the phone. Minutes later we were on our way. There was little to say. Custom dictated that any time a fire was spotted in the community, everyone converged upon the site to lend a hand in keeping the damage under control. There was no local volunteer department or emergency crew on call in the area. It was a neighbor-help-neighbor environment and no one failed to answer the call.

Spring was fire season. Dry, brittle underbrush, the legacy of a harsh winter, made open fields and wooded areas equal targets for the slightest spark of fire. Only when the spreading flames were extinguished and smoldering embers were being carefully beaten to smoky fragments could anyone begin to speculate upon the cause of the fire. A carelessly tossed cigarette from a passing car? A camper's failure to douse a cooking spot?

That afternoon neighbors were gathering, immediately attacking the fire that was blazing its way from the property fence bordering the road northward toward the woods that stretched into acres and acres of uncultivated land. The owner of this property lived in the city. His absence, however, didn't deter anyone's effort to fight the fire. All realized their own interests, their homes, their farmland, their very lives could be in jeopardy at any time a fire gained enough force to sweep unchallenged across the countryside.

Some men who worked in the city had not arrived home. Women, older children, farm hands and everyone able to wield a shovel, swat with broken off evergreen limbs, rake to clear an open path to break the fire's advance, or smother flames with a snatched up piece of canvas from barn or garage all feverishly attacked the task at hand.

My mother, cautioning me to stay in the road, crossed the ditch at a low point and walked up the steep incline on the stubble grass between the road and barbed wire fence marking the property. A sharp drop-off to her left plunged to a deep ditch and the roadbed below.

"I want to help. Can't I come, too?" I called.

"No. I'm coming down to go through the fence down the road." Looking around at me as I called to her must have made her feel unsteady in the narrow strip of space as she neared the top of the incline. Instinctively she glanced around for something to hold onto. She reached for the one thing she saw handy, but it was just beyond her grasp. One step backward should let her reach it. She needed something to help her keep her balance along the high, narrow strip of soil. As she glanced down and backward to be sure of her footing, a searing scream tore through the air several yards ahead of her.

"He's on the fence." The crying was a shriek.

"Help him. He can't turn loose!"

One of the farm laborers who worked for our nearest neighbor up the road had come with her to help. He was face down across the barbed wire fence. "Don't touch him," she cried, rushing toward the fence. Glancing up, she saw a sagging power line, weakened by recent winds and a late winter storm, drooping deep over the level of the top strand of wire but not touching the ground. As the worker had attempted to beat down the fire, just beyond the fence, he had grabbed the top wire to swing over it. In the gusting wind the charged high voltage line swung against the fence as he straddled it, instantly sending a death-dealing surge of power.

Realizing what was happening, that his body had become a helpless conduit for the electrical force plunging from the power line to the earth, our neighbor grabbed a rake and holding tightly onto its long wooden handle, hooked its curved metal prongs securely into his overalls and pulled him off the fence.

"Go back, don't come up here," my mother called to me and, looking up toward what she had been reaching for only seconds before, saw that it was an extension of the power line that slumped alongside the fence, unnoticed by anyone until the moment of tragedy.

The shock of the man's death chilled my heart. The fire we had seen and feared had been caused by a silent, camouflaged killer. With rushing awareness I realized how near my mother had come to touching the deadly power line. The thought of such a horror left me numb. I could not speak of my feeling.

Later, telling my dad what had happened, I felt every detail of the afternoon return and I was suddenly crying, shaking, helpless to do more than blurt out, "I can still see Mom starting to reach up for that power line and then suddenly that scream down the way and…"

Dad's arms were around me and he was talking to me in a calm, low voice. "I know you were terrified. Let's you and I say a prayer and thank God for protecting Mom and…" he paused.

I burst out, "The man who died, what about him?" As if completing his own thoughts, Dad said, "We'll pray that he is now safe with God." That's when Mom walked in, watched us silently a few moments, and joined us.

Bitter Test of Faith

My mother normally a very calm woman, was pacing the floor, literally wringing her hands in despair, fear bringing a pitch of hysteria to her voice and a stream of tears down her cheeks.

She took no comfort in my father's controlled voice. Thunder sounded in repeated assaults so close behind the jagged daggers of lightning splitting the blackness that it seemed the house would fall upon us all or burst into raging flame.

Reaching up to grasp my frantic mother's hand, I said, "Don't be afraid, Mommy. The Lord will take care of you."

Blowing rain beat with fresh fury against the windowpanes as the sound of thunder crashed ever closer. My mother looked down at me tugging at her arm and suddenly became motionless. For several suspended moments she stared down at me as though hypnotized by the sight of my uplifted face. "What did you say, Baby?"

"Don't be afraid, Mommy. The Lord will take care of you."

A stabbing streak of lightning slashed the sky outside. It seemed so near I pressed close to her body, encircling her knees with my arms.

Without a word, she reached down and lifted me, quietly moving to a nearby chair, the rocker in which she had often lulled me to sleep as a baby. In it we waited, rocking gently back and forth until the storm passed and the night was silent again in a rain-washed world around us.

Growing up shifted my focus on life and those I loved. I married. I had children of my own. I felt the ties of love binding me to an expanding circle of dear ones. I didn't think I was as vulnerable as I had been as a child. At times I didn't seem to acknowledge that God is the foundation of all that I am.

Often in adult life, I have needed to remember the simplicity of my toddler faith, to redeem the strength of that promise I had so innocently repeated to my mother. My faith was tested in the sudden, violent death of my mother when she was struck by a car in front of her own home.

Only a few weeks before, she had written that she at last could begin to see the "light at the end of the tunnel." She had been diligent in the months following the death of her husband, working with their attorney in settling his estate. At last, she felt things were in order. She could shed the burden of responsibility that, however demanding it had been, had helped her adjust to the emptiness of her own loss.

Without warning, she was gone. Could I have said to her, "The Lord will take care of you," as I had as a young child so confidently expressed? It seemed a bitter test of my faith, stripped now of sweet, comforting words. Was God testing me, or was I trying to blame God?

I reread the entire Book of Job, sensing anew his anguish in his losses and probing again into his search for answers from the God he had always trusted. Like the opening of a door into a newly discovered reality, I understood it was not for me to try God, but to look upon the mysterious pattern of His will with reverence.

How could I know what the future could have held for my mother? She had chronic, serious health problems that threatened to rob her of her independence. Would she have chosen a dreaded incapacity of mind or body or prolonged, painful terminal illness? My heart told me that she would not.

My cousin, first to reach her after the accident, reported that she took one deep breath, a sigh, and her body seemed to relax into a quiet peace. Could I deny that God was taking care of her, even as she crossed into a new realm?

In the wake of my mother's death, I came full circle to the truth of my earliest belief. We are part of God's plan. He does indeed keep us in His care. And it is through His grace that we can acknowledge and accept His will and purpose for our lives.

New bridge for the generation gap

The barrier that arose between us, invisible but very real, made it seem that my adult son and I were not living in the same city but thousands of miles apart. When he experienced a career jolt in a regional economic downturn, my expressions of encouragement could not change the conditions he faced. The death of his estranged father widened the gap in communication between us.

Questions haunted me. What could I say without inflaming old wounds or threatening his self-esteem? I needed a new bridge to join us on some common ground of understanding. In his growing up years, rhymes had often led to many lessons and made homework easier. Finally I wrote to him:

In a world constantly changing, I'm glad some things remain the same; and just to keep them fresh in mind, I'll call a few by name…

Success…not what others say of us, but how we feel about ourselves.

Hope…the unseen power that keeps us believing when there are few visible signs to convince us.

Fear…the force that saps a coward to defeat and drives the brave to victory.

Loss…an emptiness not yet filled with new purpose.

Failure…a way that won't work out, just short of finding one that will.

Happiness…peace within, even through conflict without.

Love…a gift of spirit, stronger than reason, that saves us from the worst within ourselves, and lets us share the best.

When the telephone rang, and I heard his voice, I tried to suppress the catch in my throat. "I'm glad you called. I was afraid you wouldn't."

"Afraid I wouldn't call?" He paused, and I heard a chuckle. "I thought you left out something. Now I know what it was…Faith!"

Suddenly I could smile again. "And it took you to show me. I hope I'm not too old to learn."

"Never."

A Chance Meeting

Battling the chronic pain of a spinal curvature growing more pronounced with age, I was trying to maneuver my shopping cart down the store aisle as best I could. Only one other cart was on this aisle. It stuck out at an odd angle, so I could see no easy way to pass by it.

Tentatively, I started to move the other cart, hoping this would attract the attention of the woman bent over examining the shelf of nutritional supplements. Engrossed, she paid no attention to my efforts. Finally, she straightened up and started commenting on the economy of the product she held over some other brands.

We began chatting. She was supposed to be drinking three cans of supplements a day. She commented, "Considering my income, three of these cans a day is pretty costly."

I told her briefly of my experience. I mentioned my delight in finding another product that I really liked, but which was much less expensive. It had long been a real energy provider for me.

Frightfully thin, she explained that she needed two major surgeries, but both were on hold until she gained some weight.

Thinking about the help relatives can give, I asked, "Do you have family nearby?" Looking up, she said, "Oh I have two sons within driving distance." Pausing, she added, almost timidly, "But you know, I don't think I can find a greater help than prayer. God is my constant companion."

At that moment, I felt a kindred spirit with her. My own trust in God was reinforced. "You are right. No greater help. Please know that I will be praying for you."

Almost reluctantly, I started to move on down the aisle.

Bending over her cart, she turned suddenly and touched my arm, her face smiling, her voice surging seriously, "God sent you to me today."

Humbled by her remark, my own pain was forgotten, considering what she had to face. And I realized that meeting her on this very day, at this very time, was no doubt providential. A shopping cart that blocked my way had become a doorway to a double blessing. Two strangers were no longer strangers, but two people bonded in the power of faith. A prayer filled my heart.

A Long Night

I could not sleep. My worry crowded the blessing of sleep into a chasm of formless fear. My body ached for rest. Conscious concern for a new problem would not release my mind to let it skate smoothly into the welcome anesthetic of peaceful escape.

The clock blinked the slow passage of minutes; I turned over to avoid its stare. After a fitful few minutes, I turned back to face its soundless reminder of time passing with no solutions easing my tortured senses.

Exhausted, in the silence of predawn, I heard words shape the lyrics, catch the flow of melody in a beloved stanza of "Amazing Grace." In the dark, I followed them in my mind.

The Lord has promised good to me;
His word my hope secures.
He will my shield and portion be
As long as life endures.
(John Newton, 1779)

I felt myself becoming a rag doll upon a firm mattress. Every muscle limp, my whole spirit gave way to peaceful assurance; my mind accepting, sustained, comforted. Repeating the words, hearing the music again, and again, I slipped into sleep. I awakened to a return of the problem before me, but I was sure of one thing—abiding confidence in God's presence, guiding me to right solutions.

REFUGE

With four healthy, robust children, the youngest entering first grade in the fall, I was now free to complete college study for my degree. Another baby was not in the plan. Then came the unexpected.

All the familiar symptoms began to make themselves felt. I sat in early morning Greek class fighting back waves of nausea. Within a few weeks I was encased in a bracing girdle made necessary because of the curvature of my spine. I was determined not to be a dropout from my classes.

My spirit was stronger than my body, however. I began to lose weight at a time when most mothers-to-be are gaining. I could not give up. Who admires a quitter? My major question was, "Will my baby be all right?" I was told that things would improve if I could eat more. When that failed I was put on supplements.

Finally, I was warned that if I lost more weight I would be hospitalized. My mother came to visit and insisted on taking me to her home. My professors kindly allowed me to complete the semester's courses through extension study.

As my mother's only child I was the center of her doting care. Back in my own home town and under the care of the doctor who had delivered my first two babies, I heard him making a long distance call to a colleague, a specialist in nutrition. "Did babies born to women in wartime concentration camp conditions suffer lasting ill effects from their mothers' malnutrition?" Not totally satisfied, he decided to monitor my progress in the hospital.

Several weeks prior to my scheduled delivery date he induced labor. An incompatible RH factor between my blood and the baby's made it necessary to call our pediatrician in to be present for the birth.

The baby was placed in an isolette. The first 48 hours would be crucial. Awakening to see the tube of a second transfusion feeding into my vein, I heard my eldest daughter saying, "Daddy couldn't believe you were smiling when they wheeled you out and we found out we had a new brother."

I was allowed to see him but could not touch him or hold him. True to hospital practice, sleeping medication was the nighttime ritual, but I was restless, uneasy, unable to feel even the release of complete exhaustion.

Suddenly, I came fully awake. Was that my baby I heard crying? Was something wrong? Don't be silly, I thought. The nursery is full of babies.

It was a time that held the flat, dull, vacant silence of those thin, quiet hours well beyond midnight, but far too early for even a hint of dawn. The hospital seemed to breathe with a common shallowness, in a state of almost suspended animation. There it was, the cry again. I had to know something. I turned on my light to alert the nurse on duty.

When she came she moved with professional ease, but her manner was guarded. She would not meet my eyes as I pressed for answers to my anxious questions. She left as quickly as she could.

After that, sleep was impossible. Where could I find any comfort? I tried to pray, but my thoughts were like misty fog and I could not focus on anything to say to God. I always packed a small Bible when I entered the hospital. This time I had failed to bring it.

Reaching out, my hand touched the handle of a drawer in the bedside table. It opened easily, revealing a

Bible. I could not think of any passage to which I wanted to turn. I just held the hard binding, lifted the cover and brushed my open hand over the pages. The delicate sheets flowed under the pressure of my fingers and the Book fell open to Psalm 91, "I will say of the Lord, He is my refuge and my fortress: my God; in him will I trust."

I read on. "Thou shall not be afraid for the terror by night; not for the arrow that flieth by day..." The verses were speaking to me. Over and over I read the psalm to which I had been led, not by happenstance as some would say, but by divine guidance I was certain.

At first dawning, still holding the opened page, I lay listening to the bustling of an early morning shift. I peppered the nurse who entered my room with questions still haunting me about my baby.

Yes, he had suddenly "turned sour" in the middle of the night. The nurse on duty had called our pediatrician. He had come immediately. In fact, he had stayed the remainder of the night, settling on a cot next to the nursery, dozing between regular checks on my baby's progress.

Why wasn't I told, I wanted to know. "He didn't want you to worry. You needed to rest."

When the doctor appeared he looked tired, but his voice was strong and he smiled saying, "He's passed the most critical time. We can't say he's totally out of the woods yet, but we'll watch him closely. If we make it through the next 24 hours I think we can begin to talk in very positive terms."

After he left I read again, "There shall no evil befall thee, neither shall any plague come nigh thy dwelling. For he shall give his angels charge over thee, to keep thee in all thy ways. They shall bear thee up in their hands, lest thou dash thy foot against a stone." Angels? I could believe that now.

I realized how, when I could not seek God, He sought me. The baby I had not planned for was a part of God's plan and through God's grace he was going to thrive.

And thrive he did, blossoming into such a strong little fellow that within six months he had surpassed any limitations imposed by prematurity. One of my professors wrote to me after learning of his birth, "Please forgive me, but I must tell you, William, I'm sure, will be a scholar." I could just picture the smile on his face as he spoke.

Prayer often seems to be asking God for something. It is a plea when we are hurt, frightened, ill, grieved or lost. It is the ultimate power we invoke for help.

But for me that dark and threatening night when I could not find the words to direct to God, it was he who opened a channel of communication to me. He led me to the message that quieted my deadliest fears, promised what I could not ask for, and filled my heart with the assurance of His peace.

That fifth baby did indeed go on to major in philosophy and often calls from his home on the west coast just to discuss some point in literature or religion, or perhaps ask for a recipe for a remembered favorite food he enjoyed while growing up.

And how well he knows my favorite Psalm 91!

KNOWLEDGE

Knowledge without understanding is like a whirlwind scattering seeds but not nurturing growth.

ONGOING EDUCATION

Life's tests of judgment come in challenges of timing:

—recognizing when to *make* something happen

—sensing when just to *let* things happen

—knowing when to be sure some things *don't* happen.

Part IV

Light Verse & Humor

When I Grow Old

When I grow old
I'll give up biking;
I'll say no to hiking
And staying up late;
I'll bow to the fate
Of pesky physical ills,
Count out many daily pills,
Learn to do sedentary things
Like knitting and watching bird wings
Flutter past the window; oh, yes,
When I grow old, I guess
I'll give up trying to stay fit,
And not mind it a bit.
But not now, still short of five score
—At only ninety-four.

Delayed En Route, No Doubt

I think that the robin
Returning in full wing
Wanted to be the first
To welcome Spring.

He swoops sharply to earth
Closely to view it:
A blooming crocus
That beat him to it!

Priceless Per Acre

"As cheap as dirt,"
I've heard it said.
Or someone is "dirt poor."
But it's due respect—
this humble word;
Of that, I'm very sure.

For when I hoe
and dig and toil,
Planting seed in every niche
To cultivate my plot of soil,
my garden
Becomes "dirt rich."

TULIP TACTICS

While they stand at attention like soldiers
At arms, dazzling winter off guard
With squadrons of color scouting the yard,
Spring slips in.

Best of Summer

      Lush rows of tasseling corn
Stalking the acres
Through vast fields;
Purple berries encamped
In tangled green briars;
Plums turning from green
Rocks to red, plump succulence;
      Breezes that swirl over
Glistening sweat of midday,
Air conditioning your skin;
      Long sunsets when the sky
Stays awake by its own light
Along a hot horizon
Until the lull of twilight
Fades into night bird song.

Pick of the Seasons

I'm convinced that mellow fall
Is the choicest season of them all.
It's too late the grass to mow
And too soon to have to shovel snow.

Definitions, Deft or Daffy

A sound mind
Is the electric current
Of imagination
Safely grounded.

Sawdust is simply the soft side of
Hardwood.

No Immunity

A laugh may be infectious,
A frown bad habits spawn,
But there's no power of suggestion
As contagious as a yawn.

Development

They're grown, when
Boys who hate going to bed,
Become men
Who hate getting up instead.

My Lesson From Laryngitis

Reduced to speaking only in whispers,
I soon found out
My children proved better listeners
Than when I was able to shout.

Back Off!

Larger-than-life moles, wrinkles;
Grins baring gums and molars;
Flaws that once were corrected
By kindly air brush-overs—

Now, with high-tech camera pictures,
And zoom-in shots on TV,
I'm given far closer close-ups
Than I care to see.

Caveat Emptor

The magic word FREE
Filled me with glee,
Until I found in fine print
What the asterisk meant.

Strictly Personal...

I'm now old enough
      To know it's smart
To let a smile
      Keep me young-at-heart.

Parallel parking I can
      Accomplish with style and grace—
On a quiet side street
      With a block of empty space.

I'm impressed by the cure
      The advertisement projects;
But I'm not sure I can endure
      The mentioned side effects.

On Second Thought

When a problem becomes unbearable
And it seems there's nothing I can do,
I've found the best solution comes
If I change my point of view.

KEEPING THE PEACE

> Better I've found
> To forgive and forget;
> By not getting even
> I have less to regret.

Index

Index

Part I   Poetry

New Vision................................11
Not By Bread Alone........................12
Behold....................................13
To God....................................14
Mary......................................15
Glimpses of God...........................16
God In Christ.............................17
Destined to God's Purpose.................18
Holy Week Haiku...........................19
HAIKU...In Spirit.........................20
Reflections...............................21
The Fence Is Broken.......................22
Path of Contrition........................23
Transformation............................24
Regeneration..............................25
Searching.................................26
Faith's Witness...........................27
 ...for the one who believes..............28
Living & Believing........................29
Proximity.................................30
Heart's Reach Unlimited...................31
Stepmother to Small Daughters.............32
Autumn to Remember........................33

Church Attendance 34
Look Up 35
Love, Unity, and Peace 36
Just as Sawdust 36
Legend 37

Part II Fiction

The Lemon Yellow Dress 41
A Light in the Night 46
A Good Samaritan 51

Part III Inspirational Prose

Out of the Ordinary 59
Hidden Handicaps 62
A Lesson Long Remembered 65
Deadly Fire 67
Bitter Test of Faith 70
New Bridge for the Generation Gap 73
A Chance Meeting 75
A Long Night 77
Refuge 78
Knowledge 82
Ongoing Education 82

Part IV Light Verse & Humor

When I Grow Old...............................85
Delayed En Route, No Doubt....................86
Priceless Per Acre 87
Tulip Tactics..................................88
Best of Summer 89
Pick of the Seasons............................90
Definitions, Deft or Daffy.....................91
No Immunity 91
Development 92
My Lesson From Laryngitis 92
Back Off!......................................93
Caveat Emptor 93
Strictly Personal..............................94
On Second Thought 95
Keeping the Peace 95